T0090571

A Book of Motivational Poetry to face Adversity
and to Birth faith in God and in Yourself

TRAGEDY INTRODUCED
ME TO TRIUMPH

By LaSean Miller

Order this book online at www.trafford.com
or email orders@trafford.com

Most Trafford titles are also available at major online book retailers.

Printed in the United States of America.

ISBN: 978-1-4269-2992-2 (sc)

Library of Congress Control Number: 2010913052

*Our mission is to efficiently provide the world's finest, most comprehensive
book publishing service, enabling every author to experience success.
To find out how to publish your book, your way, and have it available
worldwide, visit us online at www.trafford.com*

Trafford rev. 8/23/2010

 www.trafford.com

North America & international
toll-free: 1 888 232 4444 (USA & Canada)
phone: 250 383 6864 ♦ fax: 812 355 4082

Contents

Introduction

Tragedy introduced me to Triumph is a poetry book,
written by LaSean Miller, it's design is to create self
awareness, along with motivation that was stripped away
due to catastrophic events. The powerful poems create the
vision of prayer, the vision of love, every positive element
or ingredient that is needed to become the person you wish
to be. Whether you are in poverty, or locked up, a single
parent, or struggling financially,or going through a divorce
or bad relationship, better times are coming. Staying
positive, and loving others is the key. We are all different,
but yet we are all the same, we began as spirits but born
human, we are spiritual beings having a human experience.
It is that experience teaches us, it is what makes us who
we are, whether positive or negative. Within these poems
is inspiration, and motivation, dedicated to the believers,
because at the end of the road we are all, achievers.

Born 2 make me strong.

Me, the total opposite of weak,
 Strength, dedication
self respect and honor,
total confidence.
Your envious ways
 birth's myself Respect,
 your laziness
activates my dedication,
  your weakness
bows down
to my strength.
You seem to come from pure evil,
 so I escape to love,
the only element
 evil is afraid of.
You have pessimistic thoughts,
 I become fearful of your parties,
your invitation to me is an obituary,
 very sick minded.
I have confusion of a gift for you,
flowers or a cure for your hatred.
 Do I pretend you do not exist,
 or do I recognize,
it is you who motivates me,
 Not to hate because of your fatal fate,
but to live the opposite of what you chose,
see your deaf was untimely,
but your birth
was only to make me strong.
Remember: Weak actions of the mind,
lead to destruction.

Purpose

Mental incarceration
What do I look to
pray time moves faster,
when time is spent alone,
But yet, no purpose shown.
Gazing at the walls
To escape the noise
Hoping for a pause
A voice says
Strength is within us all,
I recite until faith is held
Coaching myself consistently
Saying I won't fail.
Success the only option
I put failure up for
Adoption.
The strength is in me
Time to bring it out,
Bring in the faith
And release all the
Doubt
On the road to Success,
filling my mind
With wisdom, only to
Make smart choices
listened To opinions
but drown out the
negative voices,
I stay on the path
To find my purpose.
Remember: Einstein says that insanity is
doing the same thing over
and over again and expecting different results.

2

Deaf Take a Vacation

Deaf take a vacation, you make me worry,
worry about my family and friends.
 I need them with me a little bit longer,
 like forever needs infinity, and a minute needs a
second,
time and time again. Deaf you must follow my
instructions
and realize you need a vacation, a very long one that is,
get comfortable never think about your job again,
bad life situations
you work too hard.
 Deaf, discipline is good
but you are too persistent,
 get some calm down,
try to resist it,
bother no one else,
leave my family and friends alone,
if not I'll be alone.
Question! Are we your employers,
if so you're fired,
See you in court, you continued
To work ,I see the news report
I pause now, and somehow I reflect,
We employ you by birthing disease and violence,
and somehow you detect, so smart you are with all that
intellect.
 Sex with applied lust with absence of love,
that activates and sets uneducated examples
for the innocent people whom we love.
Deaf, maybe you want a vacation, and we
leave you with no choice, with our habits of
persistent blood shed

3

and uncontrollable jealousy maybe you have no choice,
so foolish we are to feel we've been robbed.
So maybe, we need to get some calm down, not you but us.
take a second, and look at ourselves, and honor God's law.
and maybe you'll able to take that vacation after all.
Remember: Life is a blessing, our existence gives life
definition.

The Remedy.

I need help, I'm all alone,
My love left me, I'm all alone.
Many wishes come to mind,
Like, I wish I never met her at all,
but since I met her,
it's a problem without any hesitation.
  Lord get her off my mind,
I need to sleep, my only cure, hopefully only
temporary if God permits me to, therefore it's pure.
Feels like I'm dying without her near me,
when she was here, man. I thought so clearly.
Look at me, time seems hopeless, She's on my mind, I
can't focus.
 Voices say pray, pray until something happens,
man if the devil is real I know he's laughing,
unconsciously chasing my love away, now I'm like what
happen,
Where do I go from here, tomorrow seems no where near,
 So therefore, I must sleep, sleep, and hopefully I'll
dream,
and there hopefully I'll see ,
after all this time, sleep was the remedy.
Remember: Think before you react, sleep on it.

5

To Cherish

To reminisce is to cherish, and to cherish is to love,
 everything is love. The past is never lost, it visits from time to time,
by word of mouth, or the back of our mind,
Is deaf cherished or feared, the time it came and took someone dear,
we will never forget , nor the feeling of losing them,
no need to admit. Do we look forward
to deaf when it comes, is there no choice,
 or do we go in peace with great rejoice.
 reunited, no more is love lost, reality kicks in,
deaf must have been false.
We must all leave this place, the day will come,
hopefully later than sooner,
especially when you're young. Lonely days,
made it possible for company to be cherished,
see once upon a time you were single, then along came marriage.
the mind wanders here and there,
there it went and here it goes,
 my facial expression is the reason it shows.
 Seconds pass and minutes go,
 what will tomorrow bring, I don't know,
until then, keep praying , be thankful and you shall
Not parish, know that life is beautiful,
 it should be cherished.

Love Tree

2 seeds planted in the soil many feet apart,
 mixed with 50 percent soul, and 50 percent heart.
 Storms came with high wind currents,
but the seeds still remained,
the desire to coexist seems to be the aim.
Days, months and 5 years past, sprouted
from 2 seeds in the ground,
 and now 2 trees in the grass.
2 trees tall as ever, as one standing tall 2gether,
the two trees had many visitors,
whom they sheltered threw bad weather.
 Branches strong built to last, and shelters many
creatures definitely, without chance.
both branches at one time became weak,
soon to break and fall apart, the many welcomes was at
il's peak.
Spring, summer, seasons came, with hopes the trees be
saved,
in time the branches grew . Bushes sprouted out with
hopes to separate
 the two overlooked, so it's purpose was no need.
Rain sunlight and a troubled past , the
trees remain to stand strong surely built to last.
Nine years had passed, going on
Ten, the trees remained strong,
never to break again.

The Acting Spirit

The human body, just a role,
first a empty shell, without a soul,
permission granted by God who knows,
body and spirit becomes whole.
 What's the script on how to love,
 Appreciate self first,
kindness tends to get weak, apply concerns with your
health,
God, the camera man our every action is within his lens,
 all recorded, and shown on judgment day our very end
 spirits dwell in heaven,
but for now we rest on earth,
thank God I'm human, a animal would be worst.
Freewill and gender, spirit characteristics, when evil
action displays,
 is the spirit the sinner. Heavens mansion and pearly
gates,
 materialistic pretenders, some want summer and prefer
not to have the winter,
  many are hungry and want dinner. Accept what God
gives,
and explore the possibility of nothing,
combine that with zero and still end up with nothing.
A living spirit, more alive than the human body,
God made spirit to give the body life,
so accept this gift eliminate second thoughts,
because life is a gift from God,
Neither to be sold, nor bought.

Thank God for the Flu

Chest pains, runny nose, sweaty nights,
chicken noodle soup
instead of what I really like.
The flu takes over my body,
like some type of possession,
along with chest congestion.
My bed is my home,
I have someone to care for me,
 for some reason I feel alone.
My body is fatigue, the mind yells get up,
where's the energy, much work to be done, people to see,
games to play,
more Exhausted my body feels, the mind says no way.
My sickness births my appreciation towards good
health,
 eating what I desire, work out and perspire,
sickness is a blessing in disguise, a time to reflect on
your needs,
wants, and wishes and transform them into ambitions.
The flu, metaphorically ambitious,
It pressed play and the mind began to wander.
It's brought me inspiration,
without it, there would've been much hesitation,
totally cold blue,
I take this time and thank God for the flu.
Remember: A cold can be a blessing in disguise, lets you
know
You're still alive, and reminds you of the goals

My Magnet

Born far apart, but destined to cross paths,
only to challenge each others love.
until the day we pass.
Make it last we must,
 it was written, one soul, just me and you
Precious like time to a dying man,
you are a celebrity
and I'm your biggest fan,
at hand the force of love is almighty,
the closer to you I get, I'm just more excited.
Can't hide it, but why would I, our attraction is so deep
No room to deny, Feels like I'm flying,
where the state of failure doesn't exist,
similar to last year, a total dismissed.
Days and years have come and gone,
my love for you is still so strong,
if a day should come and me or you, are no longer here,
just place your bets, our souls are near,
so please my dear never forget, you're the love
Of my life, and also, my magnet.
Remember: True love is real, true love is destined, true
love is nothing more than Gods wonderful blessing.

What is Greatness?

Greatness is achieving what others are afraid to achieve.
 Fear, is fake evidence appearing real,
So never believe
 in your mind this must remain.
Maintain consistency
with what your heart desires,
keep God above all,
everything below is yours.
Gods, image pure beauty,
mirrors reveal it,
take not advantage of people, only opportunity,
for it truly never knocks
it just intervenes. A wise man will change,
 but a fool won't,
competitor challenge thy self,
do what you never have done,
 receive the amount of success that your actions commit
to.
Purchase the map to wisdom,
but who's selling you say,
this map is in your heart and soul,
 something you already possess.
Glance in the mirror, stare at uniqueness,
discover the truth inside thy heart,
you are special, chosen by God, given the gift of life,
so live it to the fullest. Live life like you
Escaped death, let it not go to waste, remain Patient,
and there my friend, you will find greatness.

What Conflict?

Conflict the Conflict,
man I must be irritated,
the sound of their voices
I hate it, hate it.
Need some me time,
not they're time,
But mine, my time
To unwind and leave
All the problems behind
undivided we stand undivided
we fall, I have to stand tall
even when I'm about to fall,
kids are a reflection,
Of your every action
 have to do things right,
so there is no question.
Brains against fist,
trouble against focus,
with wisdom
conflict is surely hopeless.
Remember: In order to see where you are going, you must know
where you are, with love and family you can go far.

I'm to blame

Time passes and time goes,
where life ends nobody knows,
When time had passed,
there was no chance,
I'm going to, telling
Myself, I'm going to,
seemed like a way to advance.
But when no action came,
Still there was no change,
it became a game,
 now I point my finger
wondering who to blame.
The name is you,
 also known as me,
 the person surly is not
whoever you want it to be.
Make I Will a action,
transforming to motivation,
Next, back it up with determination,
soon you will be going places,
and the results will be in, polls suggesting
that me and you are going to win.
Head in the game where it should've been,
 success is here, now who's to blame, as I glanced
in the mirror, I knew his name.

Partner for Life

Thank you God
for the soft touch of satisfaction,
quick to feel the heart like a chain reaction.
Eye contact lustfully worth
every stare,
the welcome signal becomes that glare,
 if you're afraid of true love beware.
Total attention and worth the
embrace, be easy,
never to let fear take the place of your faith.
 I question, Could this be the one,
for so many years my life
seemed to be missing something,
 It's you that I want
love has been found, wishing
time could run off
to see how things would end,
Witnessing no broken heart's
nothing to mend,
 kids, family, and holidays, and
many days cherished together,
never alone but together,
with Gods help forever, I'm getting closer,
so close to ending my search
I first vow to be your strength
 in place of weakness,
your doctor when sickness invades,
from dust till dawn,
and ultimately your partner,
till infinity and beyond.

Soul Survivor

A black mans fame and fortune,
how is it handled, probably
hated and plotted on,
or racist dismantled.
Young black and wise,
no institutions involved,
 knowledge threw heavens eyes.
Sorrow is all around,
in the physical and felt by sound,
years of tears are donated in gallons,
 it result's in many pounds.
Help me God,
to witness someone's pain seems worse than deaf,
many say struggle makes you strong,
I look deep down into myself
world is too wicked,
false introductions
of life as a game,
The eye of the needle
didn't accept the camel,
similar to a black mans success in society,
a huge example.
A souls search for peace and harmony,
 Stored in a black mans body, a
price to pay when you possess
such a divine property.

Confusion go away.
I stare deep into life
oh so confused,
sounds of children in the background
can be heard from many blocks.
confused about life,
Who to be, a rapper, a pianist
or a artist on t. v
creativity possess all three,
therefore anyone of those I chose,
it must have meant to be.
For me, and my family
I want the best,
money, lots of food,
Preferably, chicken breast,
what will happen in my life
what I'm destined to be.
Whatever may come to me,
I'll stay true, if I do
I surely can't lose,
Struggle is adversity is a exercise,
I'm prepared for the bruises.
education is the key, my success will display,
ready for the World,
so confusion go away.

Circle of hate

Surrounded in a circle of negativity,
which way do I go,
 I choose left or right negativity is still there,
so where,
where do I go from here.
Born with a head,
2 arms, 2 legs,
totally Human,
my anatomy
the same of those who indulge within
The circle of hate.
Hateful stares,
aggressive body language,
a stranger, no introduction to who I am truly,
 something in me they wish to possess,
strenyth, energy, and focus
with proceeds for accomplishment.
I humbly ask God,
are all men equal,
cause the heart is different, I wish
Success to all,
Those on a positive journey
just look inside, the color's the same,
 no Difference,
so there's room for change.
within the negative circle, I stand tall
I continue to look negativity in the eye,
and my next move will not be
left nor right,
it will be up,
 forever, I will continue to fly.

She Sleeps

She sleeps and I watch her,
beauty is all I can see,
her eyes are slanted
lips structured with pure perfection,
hair so silky and smooth,
she sleeps, I rub my fingers threw
Her Hair, like a touch of a cloud,
a touch of heaven,
can this be real.
Awake or sleep,
her wish is my command,
a beautiful site,
heaven at a glance,
Davinci, and Michelangelo
painted beautiful breathtaking paintings,
so sad to never see the master piece
that lay here beside me,
A angel sent from above
 Forever I continue to love,
To the very end, with you my life I spend.
Each whisper
complement's your beauty,
So amazed
a angel lay this close to me.
So sleep angel, sleep in heavenly peace,
 this is how
I feel about my love, when she sleeps.

The Search

A search for knowledge,
 knowledge of what?
the ability to get what your heart desires,
the heart is warm,
whatever you seek,
be sure it's pure.
Clearly evil is impure.
Knowledge is not to be seeked
For only a the moment,
from the cradle to the grave,
this we must crave.
By foot, by horse, by car,
along came planes, silencing the birds,
The mind extends oh so far
How'd they do it,
how'd they know,
 study successful people,
 your knowledge will grow.
Hard work plus effort equals
success, believe this,
your answers will confess,
 a confession is the truth,
 if it's the truth you seek,
what's in the dark, comes to light,
remain silent don't speak,
the brain is a blessing,
 life is a lesson,
understanding our existence,
the goal is knowledge, remain persistent.

The Stranger

I just need, I just want,
I'm really confused .
Life surely not simple,
it's filled with pain,
some say lead by example,
 no good aim,
 life is too short,
let me add some height,
remove all frowns,
See if Success is in sight,
how can I be down,
Plain and simple,
drama is excitement,
scared to promote peace,
If I don't drama
Will increase
A nice guy or bad guy,
Deep down it's the same.
Depends on your focus
Or who you try to blame
Know who you are
Always remain true,
Especially to yourself
If not
Who are you.

S.I.R (Silent I Remain)

Silence is the key.
I make them wonder,
they think about me
like the element of thunder,
 if silence had sound
my presence
would be loud.
  observe these wonderers
their actions speak
Only for itself.
Like the present condition
of a smoker
who now has
jeopardized his health.
 I stay silent they focus on me,
they think I'm so deep,
like who could I be.
 My power not revealed,
Silence, the story untold,
 like the whisper to a deaf man
with no reaction shown.
I remain at peace,
 they, remain in wonders.
 I speak at last,
and again
 they begin to wonder.

Black Beauty

My goal is to please you,
 never will I tease you,
 never can we separate or be apart,
similar to how the body needs
need's a heart ,
lips of perfection,
 blessed when my name is
mentioned, you walk and I watch,
so graceful are your steps,
glad to be at your side,
definition of a black mans pride,
along with joy, it's your love that I'm after,
 so forgetful of life's problems
they don't really matter.
Total laughter cause life is short,
each moment with you is priceless,
can't be bought, if so only a fool
would sell, at I'm mesmerized
 under your spell, black magic it
does exist, who would have ever thought
 it was all in your kiss.
God, let not love be lost,
let it always remain,
If not, find her for me,
Beauty's is her name.

Woman

Why is it, when you're not here,
 I can express my love .
Maybe rejection is what I'm afraid of.
Presently my motivation is you.
 My reason for wanting,
 my reason for gain,
my reason
for when I see my goal,
I have perfect aim.
I feel so ready, this is
my chance, you're a celebrity,
 and I'm your biggest fan. Is love
made, show me how,
reveal it's ingredients,
I want a taste now,
frugal I am, therefore there is no waste .
I must say
Real is how you make me feel
I anticipate the next moment
our eyes should meet,
for you only my heart beats,
 appreciated you are,
this is forever.
Never again will I wait
to express my love,
when I see you, it will be all together,
with open arms your love I Shelter.
 My friend, my love, my hope and dreams,
women to me u r are everything.

Define You

I must be, I will be, I can,
are my words of belief,
 achieving greatness is what I believe,
my hard work will display
the blessing I receive,
not material, but the energy
to work on what
your heart desires,
Inspiration to praise god
more for
giving me life,
in the pursuit of positive goals
I remain, steady
and strong like a locomotive train,
focus I maintain, never
losing sight on what remains,
whatever remains I make the
best of, never one time asking,
 where's the rest of, self
preparation for whatever obstacle that comes forth,
I remain ready for whatever comes first,
I must be, I will be prepared for
the worst,
if that is to come,
I'll have already had faith
rehearsed.

Racism

Who we are heredity or environment,
I reach out to understand
what darwin meant,
 is societies character based on location,
 or a past family generation,
we study animals mostly
 instead of each other,
racism separates the human race,
but the racist are
quick to put dogs in a humans place.
Is a dog a human
replacement, back in the day
it was something a black man
would get chased or ate with.
The dog would bite,
the people would fight,
 racist would act so wrong,
but would feel so right.
To run is a coward, to stay is a fool,
to remain a slave, means you're
being abused, shall I say used,
sprayed with hoses, chains
around the ankles,
Emitt till muffled and mangled,
 what must be done, we must continue to fight
until we have won,
number one since the beginning,
 unbelievers put many lives to a
ending, hypocrites noticed,
so stick together like voters, because
if not the enemy will notice, racism.

Bored

Time sits still,
the phone doesn't
ring, it's hot outside,
I only hear the birds sing,
no friends to trust,
no woman to lust
my phone doesn't ring,
 nothing to discuss.
 Hot outside,
I sit under the sun
for now I'm just sitting at home
waiting for tomorrow to come.
Time stands still,
 impatiently waits on no one,
being alone is no fun,
 can't relate to no one.
Holding in feelings
wishing I was able to tell,
hopefully there is a chance,
a chance can hopefully be
Tomorrow, filled with joy
without any sorrow, so until
then I'll sit under the sun
waiting patiently for tomorrow.

Mommy tales

My feet are weary,
nobody hears me,
my hands remain clean
because of the dishes I wash consistently.
My body screams for help,
it really needs to be soothed,
when will relaxation come
so I won't have to move.
The kids remain crazy,
forever I'm there mom,
they continue to scream
while the dish rag remains in
my palm.
The phone rings I answer,
maybe they'll have a
answer, to what I really need.
My needs must be met, right now
it's a gamble, place your bet,
kids dishes and cleaning
the phone is steady ringing,
help has not yet come, rest I am feenin, feeling
like dropping everything
making a run.
 responsibility won't let me,
my kids are my heart,
my art, my nature,
I'm mom and dad playing my part. Never
gave up, my feet are no longer weary,
I lost sight, for a minute,
but my faith, and
responsibility made me see clearly.

Fall in Love

I cherish, cherish all the moments
together we've spent, more
frowns than smiles,
 but I tell you, your frown is sexy,
cursed with pure beauty,
so my duty is to please you,
not tease you, because
a tease is not a promise,
 a promise is definite,
to be cherished
and fulfilled, like a will,
the last testament,
for your spot of fulfillment
 is a treasure, gratefully explored
and Adored by every measure,
 angel from god my reward , blessings, I
see greatness in you,
against your chest I lay,
No words mention,
the sound of your heart beat is the
soundtrack of my life,
Never skipping a beat, my love
forever remains deep,
I fallen in the abyss of love
no need to save me, just let me be,
in Love.

Proud

God deliver us from evil,
please take away the pain.
 pressure on my brain
prevents me to focus,
Grant me the ability to maintain.
Confused, what is this.
Where is the good life,
that kanye mentioned, no answer,
but I can show you a bad one,
filled with slander, a child
listening to adults argue, no father
to protect my mom,
just me by my lonesome
to look after her.
The families black sheep
that's me some say,
the evil one,
I'm like anyway.
My father comes every now and then,
 I mostly wonder who he truly is,
 contemplating on, will it be too late
death intervenes, slide by the good
halfway, pass the evil and get right between.
I speak with my pen
more than usual now,
seems as if I'm coming towards the end
and my ink is running out.
 My life and reality as child
Have to stay focused
To make my family
proud

Just Us

Love is to cherish,
water satisfies thirst,
heat is for warmth,
equal appreciation, without hesitation,
are breakups due to lack
of appreciation,
Or is it attention,
 maybe the vulgar words
mentioned.
Let's try together,
 appreciation will be of no
question.
Let's work on this now,
 tomorrow is not promised,
 not knowing what awaits
 joy or sorrow,
2gether we are
so strong,
apart I feel weak, which does the devil want,
 for us not to get along, or never speak.
 Most likely both, so let's not
give in, let's continue to love each other
like we've been.
Two is better than one,
That equals you and me
Strength in numbers like it ought
To be.

The Question

A Lifetime attraction, together,
 really is complete ecstasy,
 many days in the past we have been apart,
oh how hard it was to not have you next to me,
 you are half of my heart,
together we make a
whole ,with you I'm complete.
Be mine my love,
truly you inspire me to be better,
 a better man, your identity revealed
 superwoman is who you are,
greatness revealed, the women of steel.
I display gratitude
to remind you that, I'm thankful ,
 you are never alone,
so busy I remain, putting food on the table,
so you never complained.
So strong our love, it still remains.
Steady I go to reach out more,
you I adore, all day
and forevermore, mi'amore ,
I will stay true, only to focus on your needs,
 I bow down
on this knee, Question! will you marry me.

Change

Peace, in the hearts of many,
 but there is so many
 crimes, scared for the kids,
 even mama, stay inside.
government battles
Over property they never owned,
gods property, his home
 his planet, in which we dwell.
Respect vanishes,
finished and diminished,
reproduction, god made many,
lost many in the city,
daily and yearly,
alone we're not, like
chess, take your place,
 everywhere you turn, invisible signs
 read Gods place
Vacant land, death delivered
By the hateful hand
The sun, the moon, and stars move,
god's law is at hand,
God speaks, but many never hear his command.
 Atheist thoughts, hateful plots,
a steady promotion of bodies in empty lots.
But change we can, blessed with free will,
I tell you what to harm kill hate
Cause it kills.

The ingredient

Energy, inspiration, exercise, and love,
everything the body needs.
Disease, negativity, and hate,
everything the body needs
to be destroyed.
What's the ingredients for success
For love on every level,
for faith in every walk of life.
Energy the ability to do work,
every human has this in his grasp,
anecdote to conquer laziness,
inspiration , oprah, Obama, and Malcolm X,
with faith and God tragedy
transforms into triumph. Time not promised,
go for the now, not for the later,
if you go for the now, you will
appreciate what you accomplished later.
 Attention energizes, but
your intentions can transform,
 pay attention to what your intentions are,
 your desires will not be far.
Knowledge without actions are useless,
 confined to a wheel chair,
but ambitious to walk, if the man conceives,
there's nothing he cannot achieve,
only because he believes.

My Accomplishment

Hope is children,
what I never accomplish they will,
for I won't let them fail,
Respect your woman, anger visits us all
 recognize deception, for it is the master of it's kind.
.Son, love your brother,
 any act of harm to him is only to yourself,
Karma haunts us all,
 actions displayed partial with rage,
that's life. Do the right thing
and the right thing is your
introduction to happiness,
to all who come across your path, and
all who shall come across,
will consider you great.
 Complements shall haunt you with pleasant whispers,
 which will one day birth your true love.
recognize true love with displays of
appreciation of health, without the focus of wealth.
The best is what you will become among society,
In high demand, the hope
for every man to become a man of your character,
my son never change who you are,
a change is only for the better and you are the best.
Most of my accomplishments may not be met,
 but having the best son in the world ,
is one of my Greatest.

Little Girl Of Mine

Little girl of mine,
I love you dearly,
taken by heart, to have
your heart beat near me.
Your presence is adored,
 pretty much since the day you were born.
 Bright lights no darkness total sunlight,
like the north star, the coming of a special child.
 My little princess, slash little bundle of joy,
blessed to have a daughter,
 inspiration is what you bring,
for you the best is accepted,
diamonds and pearls and all those pretty things,
 for you my dear is the world your oyster.
 Blessed I feel daily, due to your existence,
 by any means necessary, to make that smile
permanent ,
my child is at hand, planet earth you make a holy land.
Women's definition, beautiful life giver,
a angel disguised in the form of a beautiful girl,
for so long I searched for peace,
 in your eyes I see that display
little girl of mine, your name shelters cities ,
births promises of great wonders to come,
 oh little girl of mine forever
you are my #1.

<u>Mommy</u>.

Mom, your love is more than a try,
 it's a total completion,
Harmful words towards you is a total deletion.
 You make me feel so strong ,
 you're my hero,
my night in Gods shining armor,
The heart of steal,
and the faith, to make of the fake,
truly real.
 my appreciation would take an eternity,
 an example would be, I love you permanently .
My anecdote for when I'm sick,
all I need really is your voice,
and that's it,
I'm cured, your happiness seems to be one of my life's
goal,
you kept me happy for all my years it showed,
not just around the Holidays,
 but every walk of my life,
threw sickness and health,
even days I wasn't right.
My protector, my father my friend,
I thank God you're my Mother
 forever and ever
until the very end.
Remember: You only get one mother, tomorrow is not
promised,
tell her you love her today, and later no regrets
will haunt you
okay.

Grandlove

Family gatherings cooks outs
 and grandpa's whiskey.
Those times were special,
 just to have my grandparents with me.
Grandma's spirit so strong,
with that thought
 I could never go wrong.
Prayer installs safety,
 and safety is what one needs,
grandma taught me to pray,
 and from that I believe.
They have Passed,
they live threw what I achieve.
 Grandma said when doubt comes,
 just continue to believe.
 I suffered Trials and Tribulations,
I now shout bring it on,
 I'm able to take pain like
Jesus in the bible
with all those thorns.
The time, to mourn those
of whom you love
will one day come forth,
hopefully no time soon,
 but the day it shall come,
 give flowers that bloom,
they exist still, close your eyes,
 and feel there love and bliss.
Grandparents, moments cherished,
a love never perished,
 nor never far away, in my heart, they will
always stay.

My Queen

Me and you alone in this room,
 purely cursed amongst many
options towards pleasing you.
 Maybe even a tease, that's
for what's to come,
 anticipation of a surprise,
for The moment is real,
you're the deal,
no strings attached
totally keeping it real.
 The fact is, I'm really in love,
 only with you my Queen,
 my pedestal is your seat,
my hands massage your feet,
room brightens soon as you enter,
my hearts in the middle
that means you are the center,
 What is it your heart desire's,
please let me know,
 my desire is you,
rain sleet or snow,
letters from me to you
 whispering sweet little something's,
 language of passion,
only you can understand,
like Roger Troutman, I wanna be your man.
 Bills paid, bubbles baths and special gifts on holidays,
 like burger King, my Queen
 have it your way, what's mine is your's
you I adore,
 be my Queen forevermore.

I'm the Student

A test of knowledge
not only sought in college,
to be above average
you must carry a lot of baggage.
A long distance to walk,
hands filled with chalk,
can't give up now,
in time you'll no how.
Can't stay silent,
so begin to speak,
talk about what
you don't understand,
or what they try to teach,
the extended ruler,
a measure you could attempt to reach,
high above all the rest,
Success you excrete
you could pass the test.
To be number #1 you must
forget all the rest,
focus on the most important,
which is you, always aim high,
pay attention to what you do,
but do it positively,
you're be above the rest,
the struggle made you strong,
me, myself and I,
passed the test.

Hypocrites

Beauty is skin deep,
 because I have seen it from afar,
 on the outside looking in,
 what do you find,
something you should maybe,
 or are you spying,
 up close and personal,
and personal is a secret,
 so if I tell you something,
 then you must keep it.
Cause utter is sound,
and sound we hear,
what goes around comes around
 The spreading of fear
 Hurt feeling's sheds tears,
seconds becomes to minutes,
 days become years,
time to heal,
but the damage was done,
 if there is no one to fight,
 there's no reason to run,
 why run if you caused no harm,
you can get out of anything
 where's your charm.
 Now comes the harm,
 something I didn't start,
people were happy,
but now find a broken heart,
 I'm not a crook, I promise,
 I tell you it wasn't me,
but you'll never know,
 national evil wittiness stations, the news,
 I continue to be me,

40

while everybody else snooze,
 guilty as charged with charm an a smile,
 I'm going back in the house,
oh yeah question! is the war over with now?

Rewind

What if we could rewind time,
 would you take back
those hurtful words,

when you heard I love you,
 would you do
The same in return,
I should have, I could have,
 but did not
 The space is empty,
 could have been my spot,
 A vision, in the past now,
time is missing.
 gone with the wind,
Missed my chance,
to respond the right way,
 stuck in the past in this trance.
 Granny loved me dearly,
 My actions, I hurt her feelings,
 I see that so clearly,
Wish I had her near me
Study the past notice The signs
Cause this is the present
You can't press
Rewind.

Call on Him

I'm cheating on her,
 I'm sleeping with depression,
 in the raw not using no protection.
Depression is just one,
 there's frustrations too,
sneaks in my bed
whispering in my ear,
 I love you boo.
They form together,
 now in a threesome,
it's getting hot, I'm unable to focus,
together they surround me like a
plague of locust.
I travel deep in my mind
to find the strength,
remain faithful I say desperutely
To myself, but not able.
 I shout to God, he introduces
Faith my relief, for some reason
 now depression and frustration, won't speak.
 Crawling out the abyss what a struggle,
man that hole was deep,
a lesson learned, only God can defeat,
 I left frustration and Depression alone,
 and stayed with my lady faith,
 Keep God on speed dial
and call on him
For heaven sake .

43

The devil's Whisper

Beyond the shadows
  beneath the truth
beholds a lie,
Good decisions gone bad,
chronic procrastination,
now beyond hesitation.
Eyes of strangers, births my anger,
happiness unknown, but familiar with danger,
flame in my ear, a sound so loud,
 so near, that even a deaf man can hear.
 Sounds of despair, misfortunes and mayhem.
 production of confusion,
such deceitful eyes pure delusion,
 palms against my ears,
 trying to avoid all the evil I hear.
I say a prayer,
unlike never before,
I pray for a change, nothing more.
Palms now to my side,
 prayer was my protection,
like a gun at my side,
A Reception much clearer,
God spoke to me,
 and destroyed
the devil's whisper.

44

I still Stand

I still stand,
 thru the injustice and deception
I still stand,
 thru misfortune and evil perceptions
I still stand,
 thru the racism and all that hate
that surrounds me
I still stand
thru foreclosures, lost jobs,
my faith remains
I still stand,
 when I failed at something,
 I just tried again
I still stand
knowing, losers quit as soon as the fail,
 But I fail until I succeed no late
I still stand,
when all doubts came, never I complained
just over came,
 to focus on what I intend to gain.
I still stand,
thru sickness and death, my faith just exercised,
 Love conquers all is what I realized.
I still stand,
 only to succeed,
threw it all, I just had to believe
and yet
 I still stand.

Life's Lesson of love

Together for many years,
 many tears,
throughout those years,
 love was lost,
love was found,
my love is yours,
then and now,
My angel my heart,
 my everything you are,
 so strong never to part,
growing old together I see afar.
My child and yours are as one,
two more and we still
are one.
 Bonded together, chosen by God,
to have you in my life
 to be my true love,
and my wife as well.
To cherish to hold,
to protect from harm,
Shielded from fear, no need to be alarmed.
You took my hand,
I grabbed it gladly,
I'm flying high defying gravity.
 Is this illegal I say,
feels like a drug,
you injecting me
with all of this love.
 You taught me to love,
and how to be gentle,
how making love is not only physical
 it's also mental.
Growing old together,

46

continuously staying strong,
love is great
 a life lesson learned.

<u>Ashamed</u>

Gone to soon, gone to fast,
 I stare at the wall,
thinking of the past
 days had come, all the years went,
drinking all this gin,
making myself sick.
My body yells for help,
 but my body just wants more,
 out of cigarettes,
 got to go to the store,
so that means more,
more coughing, more wheezing,
All in my head, it's my mind I'm pleasing,
 if not I'm just teasing,
so cold the Mind, it's frozen
 I sleep it thaws out, only to do it again,
right after the room completes it's spin.
 No courage, no faith, just all this fear,
I eliminate it all after
I take this pill here,
 sounds real ill, stealing from my family,
 purchase what I need,
they support all my bad habits.
 I leave it alone for a while at least
 Death around the corner I need some peace,
how do I fight this, and put it all behind me.
 God please help, ashamed of myself,
sick of all the doubts, sick of all the fears,
sick of being sorry of myself,
dehydrated from all the lost tears.
 a voice says
First ,You must call on me
 Son no need for shame. I am
the father, God's my name.

48

The Author

Struggling times,
witnessing crimes,
telling the truth
along with many lies,
old stories mixed with the new ones,
history repeats itself
backwards like 2,1.
Only to go forward
searching for a change,
while I'm looking for some change
can't remain the same.
Time holds a lot of pain,
but why complain.
Gods in control,
I'm walking with his Permission,
on the stroll.
He guides me when I praise him
so praise again,
I get a raise,
not just my bank Account,
but also my faith,
and health as well,
so high in the sky,
I see no hell.
I follow and he leads me to glory
It's like a book,
Gods the author
and you're the story.

Power of the Word

Hennessy sits next to the bible,
 both can guide you,
 straight down
or straight up
Questions unanswered
the Hennessey speaks out
real aggressive,
 the bible speaks,
peace is all out.
The bible speaks so humble,
 unlike Hennessey
 with a mumble,
 walking around stepping
with many stumbles.
What I need, verses what I want,
 peace and happiness
this is no front.
Hennessey seduction
 very intense intoxication,
the bible and Hennessey,
 Truly no relation.
The word is what I heard,
 just listen,
focus requires much attention,
within the mind are great inventions,
so change your intentions,
 misery becomes missing,
 a changed mind
with new intuition.

Eyes behind the clouds

Jesus peaks out of the clouds,
 Focused on humanity
With a powerful smile,
 from high up,
on humanity he looks down.
Spirit sees sprit,
 aware of his presence in the cloud.
Prayers travels from the mouths all,
 threw the wind that shapes the clouds
It's destination
towards the lords files.
While, the prayers travel,
 God also hears,
tears hit the ground
Beneath the devils ears.
  believers scream,
God I want change,
not the Money, but my heart from within,
 I'm tired of lying
being surrounded with sin,
answering all my problems
 with a bottle of gin.
Focused on how the world perceives me,
  instead of how I see myself,
 but not the mirrors reflection,
 but my views on myself,
resulting in rejection..
Please God guide and restore my health,
May my family see your face
within my change,
 Glory be to God,
 I won't remain the same.
Jesus peaks out the cloud,

51

focused on humanity,
I then look up
Thank God for restoring
My sanity.

The Cup of Wisdom

I drink from the cup of wisdom,
I then swallow my pride,
So intoxicated I feel
all this knowledge inside.
I began taking little sips,
next came the big gulp,
Not knowing how I would handle it.
I drank it all up
I drink from the cup of wisdom,
I now taste faith,
Oh My God the taste was great
So potent was faith,
It drained out all the fear,
many years, haunted by grief,
A swallow of faith,
a drink much needed,
I can do anything
faith made me see it.
I drink from the cup of wisdom,
I get a taste of All the love,
it filters all the hate,
Something I could appreciate
ignorance pours out my pores,
I cherish my true love,
whom I adore.
Vulgarity replaced, with I love you more
I drink from the cup of wisdom
I gain realization,
we are spirits, having a human experience,
is my explanation.
We Have faith,
we have love,
Drink from the cup of wisdom
you'll receive
all of the above.

53

Righteous Man

Oh righteous man
Your life taken
By another mans hand
Oh righteous man
Your family displays sorrow
Haunted by the thought of
Not seeing you tomorrow
Oh righteous man
See you in my dreams
Without you, reality isn't
What it seems
Continuous violence
A home now silenced
Outside I here all the sirens
Oh righteous man
Should I hate the man
That took your life by hand
Can't seem to forgive and forget
Please understand
Deaf delivered by a stranger
Surrounded by insanity
And uncontrollable anger
No sign, headed towards danger
The righteous die
the evil lies
Where's the justice
Wittiness's deny
Oh Unrighteous man
Please never kill again,
Hopefully in the end
God will understand
Why you killed
A righteous man.

Tragedy introduced me to Triumph

God take me higher pass the pain,
 Help me see pass the rain,
It blinds me constantly,
I'm going insane.
driving in the Wrong lane,
where disaster is possible to claim.
 I've grown so weary,
People are leaving the planet daily
 not only adults, but babies.
Life is so precious,
 but many are unaware,
 especially the raft of God,
 maybe they don't care,
or either believe,
 Know the devils job
 Is only to deceive.
so hard to believe,
Deaf is not hard to achieve,
 victims screaming I don't want to Die,
 the devil love's the plead.
Love each other as you would love yourselves,
 put positive Books upon your shelves.
 You are what you eat,
 and the same is for what you read,
what the eyes focus on,
they tend To believe.
Sexual videos creates the lust,
 violent movies shows the Fuss,
 positive books teaches us to discuss,
the solution to the problem
No room for the fuss.
Past mistakes already achieved,
surrounded by violence

Negativity exceeds, only if you let it,
Invite the change
become a believer,
never be afraid of change,
As long as it's for the good
 be glad to take the blame,
 doing the same thing
and expecting something different
 that's, insane.
 So Study your environment ,
As well as yourself,
 Become the master of your fate,
 Adversity shaped, threw all
The pain and the crying
You'll soon say how
 tragedy introduced me to triumph.

He Still Lives

dedicated to my father Alex Strong
He still lives, trust and know
So selfish we are admiring the flesh,
But remember the soul.
He still lives, a stranger to some
But loved by many, planting the
Seeds of life, creating plenty.
He still lives, life's no longer temporary
But now forever, a gift we all will
Someday claim, therefore each
Moment, we should treasure.
He still lives, because I believe,
 I'm aware Of the devil
and his ability to deceive,
The negative whisper, that claims defeat,
Soon he recognizes Gods image,
now he's at My feet.
He still lives, God is great, Lazarus was
Dead but God said awake,
be and it was, that's
The power of God, so easy for him,
what seems to us To be so hard.
He still lives, not in the physical,
But very well much alive,, just look
At his last name, see only the
Strong survives.

Bring Her Back

Bring her back, she's lost, and
Wants to be found
she wanders the streets with
trails of crack on the ground.
Bring her back, she abuses herself
With vices and needles in
Her arm, she searches
For temporary love, but
only finds harm.
Bring her back, she reaches
To put money in her palm,
Only to invite, various
Diseases with open arms.
Bring her back, she needs family
For that strength, God for
Eternal love, so lost
Is her mind filled
With so much drugs.
Bring her back, the kids
Need her home, they
Want to desperately search,
Unfortunately their not
Grown.
I ask again, bring her back
Home, but sadly it was too
Late, I speak to you Lord
As I stood over her grave,
Bring her back home
with you now she stays.

Tonight's Plans

My plan tonight is to achieve
The enjoyment of life
Filled with family and friends and laughter
A place where negativity
Doesn't matter.
Chase me only with smiles, hugs
And jokes, filled with deep
Conservations that display
Unbelievable hope.
Surround me with beautiful
Intelligent women, even, with
Brothers who strive for peace, with
Non-existent visions of a
World of sinning,
 a Place where killing is
Deceased, and hopes
And dreams are increased.
My plan tonight, is to achieve
The enjoyment of life,
Celebrate this night with peace,
And remain that way, even
While my drink is released,
In my glass, and celebrate
Tonight only with
Class, sincerely
Tonight's plans.

Definition of Success

Success a word mostly abused
With the display of material,
Knowledge held along
With the people they use.
So lonely the arrogant mind,
Thinking they're on top
When they're so far
Behind
Success is not a measure
Of your knowledge nor material
Possessions,
compared to Another's, resulting in
Obsession.
Success is a righteous goal
Aimed to help any who seek change,
A positive aim,
a helping hand,
Resulting in possible claims.
Prestige only goes so far when
Wisdom is kept a secret,
Behold, knowledge
 why not Teach it.
Obtaining a similar gain,
success, helping
Others is the target,
What a perfect aim.

God Made You For Me

God made you for Me
My heart is yours
So much in common we share,
My heart is pure.
God made you for Me
Such a connection I feel
Exposed to counterfeit love
For so long, I now know
Love is real.
God Made You For Me
With you I see
A blissful future
You and I hand and hand
Past relationships had pasted,
I'm yours, my love
At last.
God Made you for Me
I feel your pain
Protect you I will
Never to be hurt Again
God Made you for Me
With you I feel
So complete,
For so long something
Was missing, you
It was, and you I seek
And now you I have,
Cause God Made You
For Me.

Don't Leave

Don't leave me,
Stay Forever and a day
No problems here
Just the tears
Blinding me slowly
Dripping down my
Face.
Searching for the right words
That fit you, right now
Seems like there all
The wrong size
To my surprise.
Been a fool for so long
You threw me your love
But so foolish of me
To throw that away
Now I cry stay.
Don't leave me now
For being a fool then
I'm wiser now,
I shout to the world
I love you girl
My lady, my friend
Please don't
Leave me now.

Lost Love

Lost love, a memory is all
I have to hold on to.
Belonging to another
Mine no more.
give me back
My heart, you've
Stole it far too many times,
Feels like I'm dying
Going blind but yet
You're all I see
Haunted by vision's of
Being still in love
With me.
Switched directions, love
Going wrong.
 Be u leuder
They say, so I take the
Blame,
 what a shame
But your happiness
Is what matters
Selfish, I'm not, In love
With you I am still
I now sleep, hoping
Tomorrow
My heart will
Heal.

<u>My Heart Was Never Lonely</u>
dedicated to Renata, Kristen Laila and Nicole

See my heart was never lonely
I was a twin, inside the womb
Time so precious, its nickname
Should be zoom, it truly can fly.
25th day of July, I was the one
To live, blessed I was, can't
Tell me, life is not a gift.
For so long, I never knew just
How quite to act, no siblings.
Me , myself and I, with God, I
Would chat, the only child
For only a while, blessed with
A set of twins, lost a sister
 blessed with two more, WOW!
Big wheels, ice cream, and the
Snow ball lady, arguments
Pillows fights, Micheal Jackson
Thriller crazy, nothing can replace
My childhood, or my childhood ladies
Happy memories, brings joy and
And pain, to the past that is gone
But the love inside is what's strong
I thank God for, the ladies of my
Life, cause my heart was never alone.

Reality: Within every problem there is
A hidden opportunity

Beautiful Woman

Beautiful woman, you are
So amazing, touch by heaven
Greeted with prayer, hypnotized
Into your eyes I stare, I see a blissful
Future with the lives we share.
Beautiful woman, oh how strong
You are, nine months you held
A gift of life, inside the sounds
Of infant cries, birth to hellos no
Goodbye's.
Beautiful woman, you are a
Symbol of hope, of a world
Now that seems so lost,
Your ambition fuels
hope for change.
Beautiful womun, with u
Love so tender, you are
The light that shelters
Me from the darkness
And deception, my angel
My divine protection
Beautiful woman, I love you
Unconditionally, I thank God
You were sent to me, It could
Of been someone else, but God
Blessed me , with a Beautiful woman

Let Me

The others was about the material
I'm about love, your Well being,
my objective is to create happiness
within your heart.
Let's build a relationship with
God in our lives, no room for
Deception, only a change for
The better, going against the
Worst.
Let me produce the laughter
That will generate your smiles
To produce tears of joy, with the
Absence of pain of all degrees.
Let me, shelter you from all
Your worries, and fears, where
Trust and honesty exist between
Us like sound and vibration, where
All your needs meet no hesitation.
Let me hold you, I say I love you
But rather for my actions to
Introduce the plea of my
Convictions, therefore time will
Only real my love for you if
You let me.

Never take love for Granted

I was shown love with open arms
I was told I was loved many times
My attitude has left me alone
Where love can't be found
I had my family support,
I had the support of my friends
So selfish I was, only to be
Concerned with my well being
And not my family and friends.
My hands now reach out, only
To have no receiving end.
I had such faith in my abilities
I'm now condition with no self
Control, over my unhealthy desires
Forgive me God, have I sinned
On my knees I fall, I scream to
God my life is yours, my heart
Now is pure, I've put away my childless
Things , A believer I am for sure.
I realize receiving love, and not
Giving love back can leave you
Stranded, I now know never to
Take love for granted.

Untitled

Materialistic views, shadowed imperfections
Guarded only by material protections,
Heal this, feel this pain, lodge inside
The brain of the unknown, concealed
With weakness, while searching
For the strong.
I hear their words, but yet
The mind still wanders, and wonders
Stevie wonder, the blind lead the blind
No problem here, being placed behind,
I study the leaders, anticipating
Failure, studying their
Moves, call me the preparer.
Chess not checkers ready to make
My move, like Hennessey and
Coke oh so smooth, not ready
To lose but only to win, obama
My destiny is at the top,
Until infinity non-stop.
A product of the past
Still here, built to last
Mistakes, studied and mastered,
No need to do it twice
I have the answers
Fate never fails so I
Changed my direction
Rising to the top
Success, my selection.

68

Food for The Mind

Never place limitations on your passions,
your true passion shall lead you to your
true self this is called soul searching.

You can ensure the safety of your defense if
you only hold positions that cannot be attacked.
Interpretation: Strengthen all your weakness,
replace your bad habits with good ones.

Your future is hidden in your everyday routine,
and routines become habits. If you do nothing
everyday you will continue to do nothing,
and nothing is what you shall have.

Have perfect faith in yourself and in your own ability
to cope with any combination of circumstances that
may arise. Interpretation: Know your strengths, ask
yourself what is it you can do better than anyone else,
and put it into action, and back it up with prayer.

Never try to do big things, until you are prepared
to go at them in a big way. Also, always think
big, larger task creates the energy towards your
desired task, you tend to work harder towards
big dreams or goals rather than small ones.

Having a vision is important, King Solomon says in proverbs. He states without a vision, the people perish, without vision we tend to lose direction, our motivation our joy even our passion as well as our energy. Interpretation: In order to know where you are going you have to see where you are.

Ignorance is knowing the right thing
to do, but choosing not to do so.

We need to end arrogance, and accept the fact that there are others who are as smart and wiser than we are, if not more so seek their counsel before making decisions before placing judgement.

Poverty does not have to be our fate. Proverbs 6: 9-11 says, how long will you lie there, when will you get up from your sleep. Poverty will come on you like a bandit and scarcity like a armed man.

Our daily routines transforms into our present habits. If you are looking for different results do something different, if not you have just defined insanity.

Look for a mentor, they're great partners. A mentor is someone who has already achieved extraordinary success in the area in which we want to achieve success, either personal or professional.

Correct the errors of the past and pick
up new disciplines for the future.
Never wish things were easier wish you were better. Never
wish for less problems, pray for more skills. Never give
distractions your attention keep your eyes on the prize.

Its not what happens that determine your future, it's
what you do about what happens, but do the right thing.

if you help people get what they want, they
will help you get what you want.

We are spiritual beings having a human experience.

Whatever we focus on we give it energy, but with good
intentions we are able to transform any situations
outcome. Interpretations: Never be distracted by
foolishness, when you do, you become a fool as well.

We must continue to grow mentally and all
ways have a open mind. The mind is always on a
continuous increase. Example: Every thought we
think makes it necessary for us to think another
thought, the mind is always expanding.

In order to know more, we must do more, and be more,
therefore before you know it, you will have more.

Life is the performance of function, we live when we perform every function, physical, mental, and spiritual. Therefore if you are reading this you are alive, put life into action, and live it to the fullest.

Those whom look for a fight, trouble is not far away, those who offer peace neither is it far away, always offer peace and watch the outcome.

In order to know where you are going, you have to see where you are.

There is no such thing as good luck, only opportunity, so seek it. Good luck is when opportunity meets preparedness.

Poverty is attracted to the one whose mind is favorable to it, just as money is attracted to him whose mind has been deliberately prepared to attract it.

When you give attention to the demands of the ignorant, you leave yourself open to their influence. Therefore ignorance it cancels them out.

Only animals have set patterns, which is why we are able to hunt and kill them. Man has the ability to alter his behavior. Therefore avoid insanity, which is doing the same thing over and over again expecting a different result.

Losers quit as soon as they fail, Winners
fail until they succeed, so never give up,
there are people who depend on you.

The secret to getting ahead is getting started.

Unsuccessful people focus on problems,
the successful focus on solutions.

Don't seek faults, only seek virtue

It's a blessing to understand that spirituality
is stronger than any material force.

Thoughts are like seeds they grow, so becareful
what type of thoughts you are planting in your
mind, make sure they are healthy and positive.

Success follows those the seek improvement

Life is too short not to let, those whom we love and care
for know how much they're appriciated and loved

Similar to colds, attitudes are contagious,
so try not to catch one.

Everyday you are either repairing or preparing,
Everyday you are either trying to fix
yesterday, or preparing for tommorrow.

Look at failure as education, not the end

Wealth is great, but be thankful for your health

Don't compete with other people compete with yourself.

Time is all you have, and one day you may
have less time than you think, so cherish those
whom you love and are able to call friend.

If you can't enjoy something accept it. Like changing
a tire in the rain, you may not love the situation, but
you have to accept it as it is, and keep it moving.

You are the most important person in your life, your
good health is your most important priority, our other
priorities, such as children or family are placed above our
health. How good are we to them sick or even worse dead.

Knowledge is power, but without action it's useless.
Action unites great success, action produces results.

Nothing has any meaning except
the meaning we give it.

74

Never give up on your dreams, Be like Colonel Sanders, The founder of Kentucky fried chicken, he went around the country trying to find someone to back him up with his recipe, at 60 years old, one thousand and nine people told him no before he got a yes. He changed the eating habits of this nation, and became a millionaire, never give up.

Understand there is no such thing as fear, fear is abbreviated as, Fake Evidence Appearing Real.

Some people take a experience and make it work for them, while others take a experience and make it work against them, I say defeat adversity.

Everyone has problems, the ones without problems are those who are in cemeteries.

What you continuously hear, you ultimately tend to believe, which determines what you can and cannot do. So, whether you believe you can do something, or believe you can, you are right.

Remember failure is only temporary, the secret is to do something different to achieve you desired results.

Always look at failure as a challenge, because
as soon as others notice your failures, they will
soon challenge you, either by position, or title.

The past should serve as education, and you should
take what was valuable and learn from it.

We create the outcome of many life situations,
stay positive and focus on what you want
and not what you do not want.

You will always move towards those increase you,
and away from anyone who make you feel less.

You will only be remembered for two things, the
problems you solve or the one's you create.

You will never change your life until you
change something you do daily.

Everything God has created contains a
invisible instruction, a hidden purpose.

You cannot change your destination overnight,
but you can change your direction.
If you don't change your direction you
may end up where you are headed.

Progress is impossible without change, and those who cannot change their minds cannot change anything.

Life is 10% of what happens to you, and 90% of how you react to it.

Sometimes it's the smallest decision's that can change your life forever.

Each relationship nurture's a strength or weakness within you.

Failure comes to those who become success conscious. Failure comes to those who indifferently allow themselves to become failure conscious.

You are the master of your fate, and the captain soul because you have the power to control your thoughts.

To reach your desired goal, you must become conscious of that goal. Just as the God fearing are God conscious, if it's success, you must become success conscious.

Have your mind conceive, your hidden desire, as if it has already come to pass. If the mind can conceive you will indeed achieve it, but only if you believe it.

Turn your passion for success into a obsession,
use linebacker mental toughness, become fearless,
walk on faith, this will lead you to your destiny.

Wish for your brother and your sister what
you wish for yourself, good things.

Take care of your health so that you can enjoy
the success that you are aiming for.

laSean Miller is a educated young man with a B.S in Science from National Health Science University, and future doctor. He is also a entrepreneur, has studied life's lesson, thru adversity and expressed those life lessons with poetry. The self-proclaimed generalist , expresses his poetry for all people to gain inspiration and seeking that much needed motivation through these hard times we are now facing throughout the world. Inside this book holds beautiful poetry, that promotes new ideas and great disciplines. Tragedy Introduced Me To Triumph will increase faith in yourself, along with the awareness Of the living God who is always watching us, Even for those who don't believe, they soon shall. There are sections that deal with losing someone close to you, by Deaf or divorce or a major break up, but gaining faith in the end. The messages in the book are simple, at that is continue to love and appreciate what you have while you have it, and be thankful that you do. This book is a guide for anyone who has ambitions, goals, and heavenly dreams. This book will also bring the best out of those who often feel they are at their worst. The poems are different expression towards the appreciation of self, children and the entire human race, so enjoy my friends, and I'll see you at the top. Please understand life is a gift from God filled with love and adversity. Each obstacle is a lesson learned, a highway to heaven. So, Exercise those hard times and there you will find the map to a road called Triumph.

79